D1269243

Nature's Children

VULTURES

Tim Harris

GROLIER

FACTS IN BRIEF

Classification of Vultures

Class: *Aves* (birds)

Order: *Falconiformes* (birds of prey), *Ciconiidae* (New World vultures and storks)

Family: *Accipitridae* (hawks, eagles, kites, and Old World vultures), *Cathartidae* (New World vultures)

Genus: There are 14 genera of vultures.

Species: There are 15 species of Old World vultures and 7 species of New World vultures.

World distribution.   Warm areas of the Americas, Eurasia, Africa.

Habitat.   Grasslands, forests, mountains, farmland, towns.

Distinctive physical characteristics.   Large birds with long, broad wings, a long, featherless neck, and a hook-tipped beak.

Habits.   Active in daytime. They spend much of their time soaring above the ground. Most feed in groups on dead animals.

Diet.   Mostly carrion (dead animals), but also some live animals; some eat nuts and scavenge for a variety of food.

© 2004 The Brown Reference Group plc
Printed and bound in U.S.A.
Edited by John Farndon and Angela Koo

Published by:

**An imprint of Scholastic
Library Publishing
Old Sherman Turnpike, Danbury,
Connecticut 06816**

Library of Congress Cataloging-in-Publication Data

Harris, Tim.
    Vultures / Tim Harris.
       p. cm. — (Nature's children)
    Includes index.
    Summary: Describes the physical characteristics, behavior, and habitats of vultures.
    ISBN 0–7172–5957–9 (set)   ISBN 0–7172–5977–3
     1. Vultures—Juvenile literature. [1. Vultures.] I. Title. II. Series.

QL696.F32H36 2004
598.9′2—dc21

                                       2003049182

Contents

The sight of a group of vultures fighting over a dead animal is not a pretty one. The vultures will have blood on their heads, and their feathers will fly as they squabble over the next piece of flesh. Vultures are anything but cute.

They have cruel-looking beaks that they use for tearing flesh. They have sharp, beady eyes. And they often have completely bald heads— revealing pink, knobby flesh. But they are all big, powerful, fascinating birds. When in the air, soaring through the mountains, the giant condors—vultures—of America are among the most majestic of all birds.

Vultures can be very majestic. This is a bearded vulture, or lammergeier, which lives on mountain crags.

Sharp Beaks

Vultures mostly live in warm regions or mountains, but they are not the same around the world. The vultures that live in Asia, Africa, and southern Europe are called Old World vultures. Vultures that live in North and South America are called New World vultures. Old World vultures might look similar to their American cousins and have the same name, but they are really different.

Old World vultures actually belong to a group of birds called birds of prey. Birds of prey are fierce birds, including bald eagles and fast-flying hawks as well as vultures. They are called birds of prey because most hunt other animals. All have a hooked beak for tearing their victims and strong, sharp claws called talons for gripping them.

Like all birds of prey, vultures from Africa like this Ruppell's griffon vulture have sharp, hooked beaks.

American Vultures

There are seven different kinds of New World vulture in North and South America. The two biggest ones are called condors.

New World vultures look quite similar to Old World vultures. Like their Old World cousins, American vultures have bald heads and sharp beaks and claws. But their beaks and claws are weaker, and they are altogether less dangerous looking. There is a reason for this. New World vultures have a way of life like that of Old World vultures—feeding off carrion. But they are not actually birds of prey. In fact, they are related to storks. Storks are waterbirds with long legs and a long, powerful beak.

There is one other big difference between Old and New World vultures. Many Old World vultures search mostly in open country and rely on their sharp eyes to spot carrion. New World vultures often go searching over forests. They need a sharp sense of smell to detect carcasses under the trees.

Opposite page:
King vultures live in the forests of South and Central America and roost in the treetops. There are birds called king vultures in India, too, but they are not related.

Meat Eaters

Vultures are made just right for getting meat from carcasses. A vulture's sharp-edged beak quickly cuts through soft meat. And although its claws are weaker than an eagle's, they are quite strong enough to grip dead flesh as the vulture rips the meat with its beak.

The bald head of many vultures is good for butchery, too. With a bald head there are no feathers to get fouled with blood and other muck. A vulture needs to stick its neck into the carcass of a dead animal to get to the animal's juicy insides. Vultures that stick their neck deepest into dead animals have more bare skin on their heads than those that just peck at the surface.

This vulture's head and neck are covered in blood from a meal; that's why it pays not to have feathers.

Master Gliders

The higher and farther a vulture flies, the greater the area of ground it can see—and the more chance it has of spying a tasty meal. A bird flapping its wings uses lots of energy. Vultures are heavy birds and spend many hours every day in the air. If they flapped their wings all the time, they would soon be tired. So, once high in the air, vultures simply glide and soar for ages on their huge wings, keeping them almost still.

The problem for vultures is getting up in the first place. One way is to start off high. That is why many vultures spend the night perched high on cliffs 10,000 feet (3,000 meters) up, ready to leap off into the air in the morning. Another way to get up is to float up on a pocket of rising warm air called a thermal. A good thermal can carry a vulture up like an elevator. Vultures have been spotted over 37,000 feet (12,000 meters) up.

Giants of the Skies

All vultures are big, but some are much bigger than others. The biggest of all are the Andean condors that soar over the high peaks of South America. Indeed, the Andean condor is the largest flying bird in the world. People sometimes mistake distant condors for small airplanes! Their wings stretch as much as 12 feet (3.7 meters) from tip to tip. Andean condors are so big and powerful that they can kill sick llamas, goats, and lambs. California condors are almost as big.

The biggest of the Old World vultures is the cinereous vulture, sometimes called the Eurasian black vulture. This gigantic bird has wings over 9 feet (almost 3 meters) long and is well able to swoop down and kill small animals such as deer. The lappet-faced vulture is big, too. Even the smallest vulture, the Egyptian vulture, has wings over 5.5 feet (1.7 meters) long.

Red Heads

Most vultures have dull brown, black, or white feathers—both male and female. But their heads are often anything but drab. The king vulture has a multicolored head. It has bare orange skin on its neck, an orange beak, black-and-white eyes, and a black-and-orange head. The turkey vulture has a bright red head. The Egyptian vulture has a bare yellow face, and the Andean condor has a reddish-purple head and neck and yellow eyes. The lammergeier (said lam-er-GUY-er) even has colored feathers—orange on its belly and legs.

Young vultures often have different colored feathers than adults. Gradually, the young bird's feathers are replaced by adult ones. Young Egyptian vultures are all dark brown, but grownups are much paler.

16

Home Range

Old World vultures live over much of Africa and in the mountains of southern Europe and Asia. Most prefer open country where they can see carcasses clearly on the ground. One hotspot for vultures is the grasslands of East Africa, where up to seven kinds live side by side. Only a few kinds (species) of Old World vulture live near forests. Many kinds live in mountain regions where there are cliffs to launch from. Cinereous, or Eurasian black, vultures, Himalayan griffon vultures, and lammergeiers all live in mountains.

Many New World vultures live in mountains, too—like the condors. But other New World vultures live in varied places. Turkey vultures live in deserts, on prairies, around farms, and in woodlands. King vultures soar high over the dense tropical forests of Central and South America. Black vultures are seen everywhere from Patagonia to New England, scavenging garbage dumps right in a city center.

Opposite page: African white-backed vultures roost up in trees where they can catch a breeze for easy take off.

On the Menu

Opposite page:
This African cape vulture is feeding on the flesh of an animal that has died during a drought.

Sometimes vultures feed on eggs or even rotting vegetables. Sometimes they hunt and kill small or baby animals. Yet what most of them really like is carrion—dead animals.

Vultures are the garbage collectors of the natural world. Occasionally, African vultures move in and snack on the leftovers when a lion or a pack of hyenas makes a kill. More often, though, their food is the bodies of animals that die naturally from old age or illness—zebras, wildebeest, antelope, or anything else that falls by the wayside. If it weren't for vultures, the plains of Africa would be littered with rotting bodies. In India people rely on vultures to clean up the bodies of dead cattle.

American black vultures raid garbage dumps and slaughterhouses for food. Condors snack on dead deer, squirrels, and rabbits— even sea lions washed up on the seashore. Yellow-headed vultures look for road kills. Only the African palm-nut vulture is mainly vegetarian, feeding on the fruit of the oil palm.

Ruppell's griffon vultures wheel in the air, scanning the ground for fresh carcasses, then swoop down.

Scanners

To spot carrion, Old World vultures soar back
and forth for hours high over the landscape.
They fly high to command a wide view—and
so need sharp eyes to spot carcasses far below.
Some vultures can see a mouse on the ground
from over 3,000 feet (1,000 meters) up.

Sometimes the vulture doesn't need to spot
the carcass itself. When one vulture spies a
dead animal, it glides down to investigate.
At once, other vultures see it drop, and they
swoop in afterward. Very soon there may be
50 to 100 vultures around the body.

Typically, small white-headed vultures fly
low over the ground and spot a carcass first.
Ruppell's griffon vultures fly a little higher
and keep a lookout for white-headed vultures.
Griffons often fly close together, so there are
always lots of pairs of eyes scanning the
ground. Often, when one griffon spots a
carcass, it circles in the air to show the others.
Above them all, big lappet-faced vultures fly
alone, looking for a crowd of griffons below.

Dining Scrum

When a carcass is spotted, everyone wants in. Before long, dozens of vultures are jostling and fighting to get a bite. They gobble it down quickly to make sure they get their share. They can strip an antelope to the bone in just 20 minutes. But there is a pecking order.

White-headed vultures get in first, but they're soon muscled out of the way by mobs of Ruppell's griffons. At once, the griffons squabble among themselves. Small hooded and Egyptian vultures hover on the fringes, trying to get a chance. Then down swoops the huge lappet-faced vulture. Griffons fall back as it lunges in with its strong beak and outstretched wings. The griffons must wait until the lappet-faced has dined. This is not so bad for them, though. Only the lappet-faced's beak is strong enough to slice through tough buffalo hide—and acts like a can opener for the griffons to get the meat inside. The griffons help the white-headed vulture, too, stripping away flesh to reveal the sinew and bone it likes.

*When vultures spot a carcass, they all dive in—
squabbling furiously to get their bit of flesh.*

Smelling Out the Dead

Old World vultures all have incredibly sharp eyes so they can spy a meal far below. New World vultures have good eyesight, too. But for them, seeing is not the only way to find food. Many live in forested areas where it is hard to see a carcass under the trees. But though they can't see it, they can smell it instead as it begins to rot.

Turkey vultures are the leaders when it comes to sniffing out carcasses. When one turkey vulture smells a carcass, others soon follow it. Black and king vultures fly high over the forest. When they see turkey vultures gliding down through the trees, they swoop down, too. Since black and king vultures have stronger beaks than turkey vultures, they may all benefit. The turkey vultures find the food; the black and king vultures rip open tough-skinned carcasses. If an animal has been dead for a long time, vultures won't bother; they prefer their meat fresh.

Opposite page:
In South America black and king vultures often dine together on the same carcass. Here they are even roosting in the same tree.

Bone Smashers

Lammergeiers live mostly in mountain areas. With feathered heads, they are the most eaglelike of all the vultures. Unlike some other vultures, they spend most of their time alone. Lammergeiers don't fight other vultures for carcasses but wait until the other vultures have gone. They arrive late so there is nothing left but bare bones—and that is just what they eat.

Sometimes they eat bones whole. At other times a hungry lammergeier grabs a bone with its feet. It then flies high into the air and drops the bone on a favorite rock far below. With luck the bone will smash open when it hits the ground. The vulture can then pick the juicy marrow from inside the bone. If the bone doesn't break, the lammergeier flies up and drops it again ... and again and again until it shatters. Sometimes lammergeiers smash turtles in the same way.

To get at the juicy marrow of a bone, a lammergeier
drops it onto a rock from high up to smash it.

Egg Breakers and Nut Thieves

Egyptian vultures eat carrion like most other vultures, but they also have an unusual appetite for birds' eggs. Egyptian vultures can break open the eggs of small birds with their beak. The trouble is, large eggs, like ostriches', can be difficult to break open, so the vultures try two tricks to get into the soft, tasty middle. Sometimes the vultures drop the eggs on rocks to crack them. Sometimes they drop heavy stones onto the eggs.

Palm-nut vultures in southern Africa have unusual feeding habits as well. They are among the few Old World vultures to live in forested areas. They live there because they eat the husks of nuts from oil palm trees. They spend much of their day perched near palm trees munching away. They are also called vulturine fish eagles because they eat fish too. They are often seen walking along the muddy shores of rivers and lakes in search of crabs and fish.

Opposite page: This Egyptian vulture is using a tool—flinging a stone down on an ostrich egg to crack it.

Roosting Vultures

Opposite page:
Ruppell's griffons nest high up on almost sheer cliffs in East Africa's Gol Mountains.

Many bigger vultures, such as lappet-faced vultures, search for food alone or in pairs. They tend to roost (sleep) alone at night, too. Lammergeiers roost alone on the highest mountain crags. But some griffon vultures are very sociable birds. They not only swoop down on carcasses together, they sleep together, too.

White-backed griffon vultures roost in the tops of riverside trees. Ruppell's griffon vultures live together on cliffs in groups of 100 or more. Sometimes, in the Gol Mountains of East Africa 1,000 or more pairs live together.

Every morning, as the sun comes up, the Ruppell's griffons all launch into the air for a hunting trip. They often have to fly 130 miles (200 kilometers) or more to find a meal. By midday most are back. But if one of them returns later with food in its beak, they all look to see where it has come from. And off they go to find the same carcass.

After courting each other in the air, black vulture pairs come down to the ground and begin to mate.

Finding a Partner

Each kind of vulture has its own way of finding a mate. When cinereous vultures want to mate, pairs soar up together, diving and twisting around each other high above the trees. Male lammergeiers perform all kinds of aerobatics—diving, swooping, and screaming past their cliff-top nests.

In the Americas king vultures circle around each other on the ground, flapping their wings and whistling. Black vultures dive and chase each other in the air. Turkey vultures grunt and hiss at each other. They may also climb into the air and grapple with their talons.

Most spectacular of all, perhaps, is the male Andean condor. He shows off to a female by rearing up, spreading his giant wings, and strutting back and forth, making a hoarse "tok-tok" call. His red head may even turn bright yellow. The male condor finishes off his display by wheeling all the way around to show off the white patches on his wings.

Eggs and Nests

Vultures' nests vary considerably. Turkey vultures are content with just a rocky ledge, a ledge on a building, or a hole in a cliff. Condors and lammergeiers make scanty nests on high mountain crags. Lappet-faced vultures, on the other hand, build a massive platform of branches on the flat top of a thorn tree. The nest may be 9 feet (2.5 meters) across and almost 3 feet (1 meter) thick.

Once the nest is built, female vultures lay just one egg a year. Turkey vultures sometimes lay two. Female condors lay just a single egg every other year. Newly laid eggs have to be incubated—kept cosy and warm—until ready to hatch. With some vultures mom sits on the egg most of the time, while dad goes off to find food. With cinereous vultures mom sits on the egg at night, while dad is roosting elsewhere. Then at dawn dad comes back with a loud roar and takes over for the day shift. After 42 to 56 days the egg hatches, and out comes the little baby vulture.

Growing Up

Baby vultures are born with their eyes open and with a covering of soft, downy feathers. At first, the parents feed the babies with partly digested food, which they cough up, or regurgitate. This food looks a little like human baby food and is easy for the babies to swallow. When the young are older, they can be fed small pieces of meat brought to them by their parents.

Baby turkey vultures can fly within 10 weeks or so, but most vultures are slow learners. Young Andean condors do not learn to fly until they are about six months old. The parents have to be very caring. Andean condor moms and dads look after their chick for up to a year until it can take care of itself. A young condor does not breed until it is at least seven years old.

Opposite page: When they are first born, baby vultures—like this 12-day-old turkey vulture—are covered in soft down.

Vulture Queues

Opposite page:
Every fall turkey vultures have to fly far south to warmer places to avoid the hard times of winter.

Most vultures live all their lives in hot parts of the world where there is always a good supply of food. Some live in places that are much colder in the winter. In summer some turkey vultures live in the northern United States and parts of Canada, but it gets ice-cold there in winter. So, many turkey vultures fly thousands of miles to the south, where it is warmer, and they can find food.

Flying this far could be tiring for such a big bird. But they look for rising currents of warm air called thermals. They float up and up. Then they glide gently away for a few miles before being lifted by another thermal. That way the birds can cover long distances with little effort. But they find it hard to cross wide stretches of water. They always cross at the narrowest point. Sometimes thousands line up to cross in the same place. The lines can be spectacular. One fall people counted almost one million turkey vultures as they soared over the Panama Canal in Central America.

Vultures and People

People have told stories about vultures for thousands of years. An old story in Hausaland, Africa, says that hooded vultures lay two eggs, one of which hatches into a fly. That was probably because there are so many flies around the dead animals that the vultures eat. Thousands of years ago, when kings called pharaohs ruled Egypt, dead griffon vultures and lappet-faced vultures were often put in the tombs of important people. The Egyptians' goddess of childbirth, Nekhebet, was said to have the body of a vulture.

In North America many ancient paintings of condors are found in caves. Native Americans used condor feathers in ritual ceremonies. At one time some people in South America thought the giant Andean condor had magical powers. This vulture is the symbol of Peru. It also appears in the art of several other South American countries.

Opposite page: *Vultures were revered by the ancient Egyptians of Africa. This ancient Egyptian frieze shows a vulture with the god Osiris.*

Back from the Brink

Opposite page:
The majestic California condor is one of the rarest birds in the world. Great efforts are being made to save it from dying out altogether.

Condors are very large vultures. There are two types: the California condor and the Andean condor. Both are rare, but the California condor is very rare indeed.

In 1982 there were only 21 California condors in the whole world. It seemed they would die out completely unless something was done to save them. So experts captured all the surviving wild condors. The captive condors were kept safely in reserves. Some even mated, and several baby condors were hatched. In 1992 some of these baby condors were set free near the Mount Pinos area of southern California. By 2002 there were 57 condors in the wild and 184 altogether—still not many, but a lot more than there had been.

A similar program is taking place in South America to help the few thousand Andean condors that live there.

Vulture Plague

Ten years ago vultures such as the white-rumped and cinereous vultures were common all over India. Some experts even thought there may be more white-rumped vultures than any other bird of prey in the world. Many people in India are Hindus and won't eat the meat of cattle. They relied on the vultures to clean up the carcasses of cattle that died.

Then in the late 1990s it all went wrong. Over 95 percent of all white-rumped vultures died in just a few years. Cinereous and slender-billed vultures suffered almost as much. All of a sudden there were dead cows lying all over the place, uneaten by the vultures. The Indian government had to set up special plants to dispose of the carcasses.

No one knows quite why the vultures are dying off. Many experts think it is a kidney infection. People have seen vultures wobbling on branches, then falling off dead. The search for a cure is on.

Words to Know

Carcass The body of a dead animal.

Carrion The rotting flesh of a dead animal that may be eaten by scavengers such as vultures.

Courtship The way male and female birds and other animals attract each other before mating.

Digest To break down food inside the body so that it can be used by the animal.

Fertilization The joining of a sperm (male sex cell) and egg (female sex cell) to make a single cell that will grow into a unique individual.

Herbivore An animal that eats only plant matter.

Mate To produce young.

Molt When a bird sheds its old feathers for replacement by new ones.

Plumage A bird's feathers.

Prey The animals that another animal eats.

Regurgitate Cough up undigested food to feed young.

Species A particular type of animal.

Talon A sharp claw on the toe of a vulture or bird of prey.

Thermal An upward moving current of warm air. Vultures use it to carry them upward.

INDEX

Cover Photo: Still Pictures: Roland Seitre

Photo Credits: Ardea: Ferrero-Labat 11, François Gohier 45, Nick Gordon 26, M. Watson 22, Jim Zipp 38, 41; Bruce Coleman: Rod Williams 7, Gunter Ziesler 14/15; Corbis: Gianni Dagli Orti 42; NHPA: Martin Harvey 21, Gerard Lacz 25, Christophe Ratier 33; Oxford Scientific Films: Alain Christof 30, Lon E. Lauber 17, Stan Osolinski 34; Photodisc: Jeremy Woodhouse 29; Still Pictures: Roger de la Harpe 4, Nigel J. Dennis 18, Roland Seitre 8, Norbert Wu 36.